AMERICAN CHRISTMAS

Edited by
Webster Schott & Robert J. Myers

AMERICAN CHRISTMAS

Second Edition

Hallmark Cards, Incorporated
Kansas City, Missouri, 1967

A complete list of acknowledgements appears
at the end of this book.

TABLE OF CONTENTS

William Cullen Bryant

THE STAR OF BETHLEHEM

As shadows cast by cloud and sun
　　Flit o'er the summer grass,
So, in thy sight, Almighty One!
　　Earth's generations pass.

And while the years, an endless host,
　　Come pressing swiftly on,
The brightest names that earth can boast
　　Just glisten, and are gone.

Yet doth the Star of Bethlehem shed
　　A lustre pure and sweet;
And still it leads, as once it led,
　　To the Messiah's feet.

And deeply, at this later day,
　　Our hearts rejoice to see
How children, guided by its ray,
　　Come to the Saviour's knee.

O Father, may that Holy Star
　　Grow every year more bright,
And send its glorious beam afar
　　To fill the world with light.

Henry Wadsworth Longfellow,

CHRISTMAS CAROL

When Christ was born in Bethlehem,
'T was night, but seemed the noon of day;
 The stars, whose light
 Was pure and bright,
Shone with unwavering ray;
But one, one glorious star
Guided the Eastern Magi from afar.

Then peace was spread throughout the land;
The lion fed beside the tender lamb;
 And with the kid,
 To pasture led,
 The spotted leopard fed;
In peace, the calf and bear,
The wolf and lamb reposed together there.

As shepherds watched their flocks by night,
An angel, brighter than the sun's own light,
 Appeared in air,
 And gently said,
 Fear not,— be not afraid,
For lo! beneath your eyes,
Earth has become a smiling paradise.

*Translated from one of the Neopolitan
Pastorali de' Zampognari*

John Greenleaf Whittier

A CHRISTMAS CARMEN

I

Sound over all waters, reach out from all lands,
The chorus of voices, the clasping of hands;
Sing hymns that were sung by the stars of the morn,
Sing songs of the angels when Jesus was born!
    With glad jubilations
    Bring hope to the nations!
The dark night is ending and dawn has begun:
Rise, hope of the ages, arise like the sun,
    All speech flow to music, all hearts beat as one!

II

Sing the bridal of nations! with chorals of love
Sing out the war-vulture and sing in the dove,
Till the hearts of the peoples keep time in accord,
And the voice of the world is the voice of the Lord!
    Clasp hands of the nations
    In strong gratulations:
The dark night is ending and dawn has begun;
Rise, hope of the ages, arise like the sun,
    All speech flow to music, all hearts beat as one!

III

Blow, bugles of battle, the marches of peace;
East, west, north, and south let the long quarrel cease:
Sing the song of great joy that the angels began,
Sing of glory to God and of good-will to man!
    Hark! joining in chorus

The heavens bend o'er us!
The dark night is ending and dawn has begun;
Rise, hope of the ages, arise like the sun,
All speech flow to music, all hearts beat as one!

Josiah Gilbert Holland

A CHRISTMAS CAROL

There's a song in the air!
There's a star in the sky!
There's a mother's deep prayer
And a baby's low cry!
    And the star rains its fire while the Beautiful sing,
    For the manger of Bethlehem cradles a king.

There's a tumult of joy
O'er the wonderful birth,
For the virgin's sweet boy
Is the Lord of the earth,
    Ay! the star rains its fire and the Beautiful sing,
    For the manger of Bethlehem cradles a king.

In the light of that star
Lie the ages impearled;
And that song from afar
Has swept over the world.
    Every hearth is aflame, and the Beautiful sing,
    In the homes of the nations that Jesus is King.

We rejoice in the light,
And we echo the song
That comes down through the night
From the heavenly throng.
    Ay! we shout to the lovely evangel they bring,
    And we greet in His cradle our Saviour and King.

James Russell Lowell

A CHRISTMAS CAROL
*For the Sunday-school Children of the
Church of the Disciples*

"What means this glory round our feet,"
    The Magi mused, "more bright than morn?"
And voices chanted clear and sweet,
    "Today the Prince of Peace is born!"

"What means that star," the Shepherds said,
    "That brightens through the rocky glen?"
And angels, answering overhead,
    Sang, "Peace on earth, good-will to men!"

'T is eighteen hundred years and more
    Since those sweet oracles were dumb;
We wait for Him, like them of yore;
    Alas, He seems so slow to come!

But it was said, in words of gold
    No time or sorrow e'er shall dim,
That little children might be bold
    In perfect trust to come to Him.

All round about our feet shall shine
    A light like that the wise men saw,
If we our loving wills incline
    To that sweet Life which is the Law.

14

So shall we learn to understand
    The simple faith of shepherds then,
And, clasping kindly hand in hand,
    Sing, "Peace on earth, good-will to men!"

And they who do their souls no wrong,
    But keep at eve the faith of morn,
Shall daily hear the angel-song,
    "To-day the Prince of Peace is born!"

Emily Dickinson

CHRIST'S BIRTHDAY

The Savior must have been
A docile Gentleman
To come so far, so cold a day
For little fellowmen.

The road to Bethlehem
Since He and I were boys
Was leveled, but for that 'twould be
A rugged billion miles.

Richard Watson Gilder

A CHRISTMAS HYMN

Tell me what is this innumerable throng
Singing in the heavens a loud angelic song?
These are they who come with swift and shining feet
From round about the throne of God the Lord of Light to greet.

O, who are these that hasten beneath the starry sky,
As if with joyful tidings that through the world shall fly?
The faithful shepherds these, who greatly were afeared
When, as they watched their flocks by night, the heavenly host appeared.

Who are these that follow across the hills of night
A star that westward hurries along the fields of light?
Three wise men from the east who myrrh and treasure bring
To lay them at the feet of him their Lord and Christ and King.

What babe new-born is this that in a manger cries?
Near on her bed of pain his happy mother lies?
O, see! the air is shaken with white and heavenly wings—
This is the Lord of all the earth, this is the King of Kings.

Tell me, how may I join in this holy feast
With all the kneeling world, and I of all the least?
Fear not, O faithful heart, but bring what most is meet:
Bring love alone, true love alone, and lay it at his feet.

17

James Whitcomb Riley

THE CHRISTMAS LONG AGO

Come, sing a hale Heigh-ho
   For the Christmas long ago!—
When the old log-cabin homed us
   From the night of blinding snow,
   Where the rarest joy held reign,
   And the chimney roared amain,
With the firelight like a beacon
   Through the frosty window-pane.

Ah! the revel and the din
   From without and from within,
The blend of distant sleigh-bells
   With the plinking violin;
   The muffled shrieks and cries—
   Then the glowing cheeks and eyes—
The driving storm of greetings,
   Gusts of kisses and surprise.

Eugene Field

CHRISTMAS EVE

Oh hush thee, little Dear-my-soul,
 The evening shades are falling,—
Hush thee, my dear, dost thou not hear
 The voice of the Master calling?

Deep lies the snow upon the earth,
 But all the sky is ringing
With joyous song, and all night long
 The stars shall dance, with singing.

Oh hush thee, little Dear-my-soul,
 And close thine eyes in dreaming,
And angels fair shall lead thee where
 The singing stars are beaming.

A shepherd calls his little lambs,
 And he longeth to caress them;
He bids them rest upon his breast,
 That his tender love may bless them.

So hush thee, little Dear-my-soul,
 Whilst evening shades are falling,
And above the song of the heavenly throng
 Thou shalt hear the Master calling.

Edwin Markham

THE SONG OF THE MAGI

*"Now when Jesus was born in Bethlehem . . . behold, there came wise
men from the east to Jerusalem. . . . And, lo, the star, which they saw
in the east, went before them, till it came and stood over where the
young child was. . . . And being warned of God in a dream . . . they
departed into their own country another way."*— Matthew

With a burning in our spirits, with a lifting of our hands,
We have threaded fallen kingdoms long forgotten in the sands—
Dead kingdoms where the thistles crowd to guard the empty
    thrones,
Where lone owls hoot their loud disdain among the scattered
    stones.
We passed the ghost of Nineveh upon the windy waste,
Where once the Angel of the Sword the paths of Eden paced.
We trod on crumbled Babylon, where once on towered hight
Her wingéd lions watched away the lone Assyrian night.
Out of the hush of the holy East, out of the night of old,
We seek the One the keepers of the sacred fire foretold.
Long centuries the wise have watched upon a peak afar,
Twelve Magi keeping vigil for the rising of the star.
Long ages they have waited for the herald of the birth,
The great hour when a Child should rise to poise the shaken
    earth.

We come commanded by a star and sent by dream we go;
Yet of this hour hereafter all the worlds and heavens shall know.
This is the One we worship in the splendor of the fire:
He is the dream of every heart, he is the world's desire.
The prophet watchers cried of him with vision-lighted eyes:

They saw his scepter hush the earth and lean against the skies.
'Twas he the Vedic poets sang in ages that are gone,
The fair young God they knelt to in the brightness of the dawn.
This is the Golden Child that rose when worlds began to be,
And floated in the lotus flower upon the mother Sea.
This is the Child of Mystery drawn down to earthly years,
To bear the common burden and to taste of mortal tears.

Lizette Woodworth Reese

A CHRISTMAS FOLK SONG

The little Jesus came to town;
The wind blew up, the wind blew down;
Out in the street the wind was bold;
Now who would house Him from the cold?

Then opened wide a stable door,
Fair were the rushes on the floor;
The Ox put forth a hornèd head;
"Come, little Lord, here make Thy bed."

Uprose the Sheep were folded near:
"Thou Lamb of God, come, enter here."
He entered there to rush and reed,
Who was the Lamb of God indeed.

The little Jesus came to town;
With ox and sheep He laid Him down;
Peace to the byre, peace to the fold,
For they housed Him from the cold!

Katharine Lee Bates

THE LAME SHEPHERD

Slowly I followed on,
Stumbling and falling.
All the air sparkled;
All the air sung.
Even to my dull heart
Glory was calling.
Slowly I followed on,
Stumbling and falling.

Great wings arched over me,
Purple and amber;
Night was all color,
Night was all gleam.
Wearily up the hill
Needs must I clamber,
Though wings arched over me,
Purple and amber.

Proudly the chorus pealed
While I was panting.
Winds were all music,
Voices all praise.
Brooks, birds, the waving trees
Joined in the chanting.
Proudly the chorus pealed
While I was panting.

Late came my aching feet,
Late to the manger;

All slept in silence,
All dreamed in dusk
Under the same dear stars,
No star a stranger.
Late came my aching feet,
Late to the manger.

Kissing a baby's hand,
Painfully kneeling,
Sweet little drowsy hand,
Honey of heaven,
Swift through my twisted limbs
Glowed a glad healing.
Kissing a baby's hand,
Kissing and healing.

Langdon E. Mitchell

CAROL

Mary, the mother, sits on the hill,
And cradles Child Jesu, that lies so still;
She cradles Child Jesu, that sleeps so sound,
And the little wind blows the song around.

The little wind blows the mother's words,
"Ei, Jesu, ei," like the song of birds;
"Ei, Jesu, ei," I heard it still,
As I lay asleep at the foot of the hill.

"Sleep, Babe, sleep, mother watch doth keep,
Ox shall not hurt Thee, nor ass, nor sheep;
Dew falls sweet from Thy Father's sky
Sleep, Jesu, sleep! ei, Jesu, ei."

Robert Frost

TO A YOUNG WRETCH
(Boethian)

As gay for you to take your father's ax
As take his gun—rod—to go hunting—fishing.
You nick my spruce until its fiber cracks,
It gives up standing straight and goes down swishing.
You link an arm in its arm and you lean
Across the light snow homeward smelling green.

I could have bought you just as good a tree
To frizzle resin in a candle flame,
And what a saving 'twould have meant to me.
But tree by charity is not the same
As tree by enterprise and expedition.
I must not spoil your Christmas with contrition.

It is your Christmases against my woods.
But even where thus opposing interests kill,
They are to be thought of as opposing goods
Oftener than as conflicting good and ill;
Which makes the war god seem no special dunce
For always fighting on both sides at once.

And though in tinsel chain and popcorn rope,
My tree a captive in your window bay
Has lost its footing on my mountain slope
And lost the stars of heaven, may, oh, may
The symbol star it lifts against your ceiling
Help me accept its fate with Christmas feeling.

Carl Sandburg

STAR SILVER

The silver of one star
Plays cross-lights against pine green.

And the play of this silver
Crosswise against the green
Is an old story… thousands of years.

And sheep raisers on the hills by night
Watching the wooly four-footed ramblers,
Watching a single silver star —
Why does the story never wear out?

And a baby slung in a feed-box
Back in a barn in a Bethlehem slum,
A baby's first cry mixing with the crunch
Of a mule's teeth on Bethlehem Christmas corn,
Baby fists softer than snowflakes of Norway,
The vagabond mother of Christ
And the vagabond men of wisdom,
All in a barn on a winter night,
And a baby there in swaddling clothes on hay —
Why does the story never wear out?

The sheen of it all
Is a star silver and a pine green
For the heart of a child asking a story,
The red and hungry, red and hankering heart
Calling for cross-lights of silver and green.

27

Don Marquis

THE BIRTH

There is a legend that the love of God
So quickened under Mary's heart it wrought
Her very maidenhood to holier stuff....
However that may be, the birth befell
Upon a night when all the Syrian stars
Swayed tremulous before one lordlier orb
That rose in gradual splendor,
Paused,
Flooding the firmament with mystic light,
And dropped upon the breathing hills
A sudden music
Like a distillation from its gleams;
A rain of spirit and a dew of song!

Vachel Lindsay

STAR OF MY HEART

Star of my heart, I follow from afar.
Sweet Love on high, lead on where shepherds are,
Where Time is not, and only dreamers are.
Star from of old, the Magi-Kings are dead
And a foolish Saxon seeks the manger-bed.
O lead me to Jehovah's child
Across this dreamland lone and wild,
Then I will speak this prayer unsaid,
And kiss his little haloed head —
"My star and I, we love thee, little child."

Except the Christ be born again to-night
In dreams of all men, saints and sons of shame,
The world will never see his kingdom bright.
Star of all hearts, lead onward thro' the night
Past death-black deserts, doubts without a name,
Past hills of pain and mountains of new sin
To that far sky where mystic births begin,
Where dreaming ears the angel-song shall win.
Our Christmas shall be rare at dawning there,
And each shall find his brother fair,
Like a little child within:
All hearts of the earth shall find new birth
And wake, no more to sin.

William Carlos Williams

As the wise men of old brought gifts
 guided by a star
  to the humble birthplace

of the god of love,
 the devils
  as an old print shows
retreated in confusion.

 What could a baby know
  of gold ornaments
or frankincense and myrrh,
 of priestly robes
  and devout genuflections?

But the imagination
 knows all stories
  before they are told
and knows the truth of this one
 past all defection

The rich gifts
 so unsuitable for a child
  though devoutly proffered,
stood for all that love can bring.
 The men were old
  how could they know

of a mother's needs

or a child's
appetite?

But as they kneeled
the child was fed.
They saw it
and
gave praise!
A miracle

had taken place,
hard gold to love,
a mother's milk!
before
their wondering eyes.

The ass brayed
the cattle lowed.
It was their nature.
All men by their nature give praise.
It is all
they can do.

The very devils
by their flight give praise.
What is death,
beside this?
Nothing. The wise men
came with gifts

and bowed down
to worship
this perfection.

Sara Teasdale

CHRISTMAS CAROL

The kings they came from out the south,
    All dressed in ermine fine;
They bore Him gold and chrysoprase,
    And gifts of precious wine.

The shepherds came from out the north,
    Their coats were brown and old;
They brought Him little new-born lambs—
    They had not any gold.

The wise men came from out the east,
    And they were wrapped in white;
The star that led them all the way
    Did glorify the night.

The angels came from heaven high,
    And they were clad with wings;
And lo, they brought a joyful song
    The host of heaven sings.

The kings they knocked upon the door,
    The wise men entered in,
The shepherds followed after them
    To hear the song begin.

The angels sang through all the night
    Until the rising sun,
But little Jesus fell asleep
    Before the song was done.

Louis Untermeyer

FOR ANOTHER BIRTH

The miracle is now. The place is here.
    No angel's wings. No throne. No diadem.
Yet, in this hour locked and rocked with fear,
    A birth may mark another Bethlehem.

No kings surround a cradle. Crowds roar by.
    The shepherds have been missing since the war.
Yet darkness splinters as a wintry sky
    Unfolds and holds—again—a burning star.

This is a time for wonders. The world cries
    For revelation, for another birth.
Dry sticks burst into blossom; dead bones rise;
    And prophets whisper to a desperate earth.

Some child unborn may rescue us, for still
    The wise men come with promise of release:
The myrrh of hope, the gold of men's good will,
    The fresh and precious frankincense of peace.

Welcome all saints, all saviors of all time.
    Welcome the thorns on every martyr's brow.
Welcome the cross. Welcome the long, slow climb.
    The place is here. The miracle is now.

Joyce Kilmer

GATES AND DOORS
A Ballad of Christmas Eve

There was a gentle hostler
   (And blessèd be his name!)
He opened up the stable
   The night Our Lady came.
Our Lady and Saint Joseph,
   He gave them food and bed,
And Jesus Christ has given him
   A glory round his head.

So let the gate swing open
   However poor the yard,
Lest weary people visit you
   And find their passage barred;
Unlatch the door at midnight
   And let your lantern's glow
Shine out to guide the traveler's feet
   To you across the snow.

There was a courteous hostler
   (He is in Heaven tonight,)
He held Our Lady's bridle
   And helped her to alight.
He spread clean straw before her
   Whereon she might lie down,
And Jesus Christ has given him
   An everlasting crown.

Unlock the door this evening
    And let your gate swing wide,
Let all who ask for shelter
    Come speedily inside.
What if your yard be narrow?
    What if your house be small?
There is a Guest is coming
    Will glorify it all.

There was a joyous hostler
    Who knelt on Christmas morn
Beside the radiant manger
    Wherein his Lord was born.
His heart was full of laughter,
    His soul was full of bliss
When Jesus, on His Mother's lap,
    Gave him His hand to kiss.

Unbar your heart this evening
    And keep no stranger out,
Take from your soul's great portal
    The barrier of doubt.
To humble folk and weary
    Give hearty welcoming,
Your breast shall be tomorrow
    The cradle of a King.

Elizabeth Madox Roberts

CHRISTMAS MORNING

If Bethlehem were here today,
Or this were very long ago,
There wouldn't be a winter time
Nor any cold or snow.

I'd run out through the garden gate,
And go down along the pasture walk;
And off beside the cattle barns
I'd hear a kind of gentle talk.

I'd move the heavy iron chain
And pull away the wooden pin;
I'd push the door a little bit
And tiptoe very softly in.

The pigeons and the yellow hens
And all the cows would stand away;
Their eyes would open wide to see
A lady in the manger hay,

If this were very long ago
And Bethlehem were here today.

And Mother held my hand and smiled —
I mean the lady would — and she
Would take the woolly blankets off
Her little boy so I could see.

36

His shut-up eyes would be asleep,
And he.would look like our John,
And he would be all crumpled too,
And have a pinkish color on.

I'd watch his breath go in and out.
His little clothes would all be white.
I'd slip my finger in his hand
To feel how he could hold it tight.

And she would smile and say,"Take care,"
The mother, Mary, would,"Take care,"
And I would kiss his little hand
And touch his hair.

While Mary put the blankets back,
The gentle talk would soon begin.
And when I'd tiptoe softly out
I'd meet the wise men going in.

Robinson Jeffers

ONLY AN HOUR

For an hour on Christmas Eve
And again on the holy day
Seek the magic of past time,
From this present turn away.
Dark through our day,
Light is the snow on the hawthorn bush
And the ox knelt down at midnight.

Only an hour, only an hour
From wars and confusions turn away
To the islands of old time
When the world was simple and gay,
Or so we say,
And light lay the snow on the green holly,
The tall oxen knelt at midnight

Caesar and Herod shared the world,
Sorrow over Bethlehem lay,
Iron the empire, brutal the time,
Dark was that day,
Light lay the snow on the mistletoe berries
And the ox knelt down at midnight.

Sister M. Madeleva, C.S.C.

PERENNIAL

The final wild song of Your birth-night
    can never be written;
The last shining word of Your coming
    can not be said.
Rough, slow-minded shepherds will run,
    angel-driven, forever
By night to a cave and a cattle shed.

And You, beyond bondage of time, without
    end or beginning,
Will wake in the arms of a maid,
    on an unending night.
You the unuttered Word become Flesh
    and forever now spoken,
Will be here, be our Life, our
    accessible Light.

Tonight is Your night, Your incredible,
    song-spangled story.
We shepherds and flocks wait on fields
    beyond Bethlehem plain;
O angels, O shepherds, O Joseph, O Mary,
    O Jesus,
O God, tell Your children the story again!

T.S. Eliot
JOURNEY OF THE MAGI

'A cold coming we had of it,
Just the worst time of the year
For a journey, and such a long journey:
The ways deep and the weather sharp,
The very dead of winter.'
And the camels galled, sore-footed, refractory,
Lying down in the melting snow.
There were times we regretted
The summer palaces on slopes, the terraces,
And the silken girls bringing sherbet.
Then the camel men cursing and grumbling
And running away, and wanting their liquor and women,
And the night-fires going out, and the lack of shelters,
And the cities hostile and the towns unfriendly
And the villages dirty and charging high prices:
A hard time we had of it.
At the end we preferred to travel all night,
Sleeping in snatches,
With the voices singing in our ears, saying
That this was all folly.

   Then at dawn we came down to a temperate valley,
Wet, below the snow line, smelling of vegetation;
With a running stream and a water-mill beating the darkness,
And three trees on the low sky,
And an old white horse galloped away in the meadow.
Then we came to a tavern with vine-leaves over the lintel,
Six hands at an open door dicing for pieces of silver,
And feet kicking the empty wine-skins.

But there was no information, and so we continued
And arrived at evening, not a moment too soon
Finding the place; it was (you may say) satisfactory.

  All this was a long time ago, I remember,
And I would do it again, but set down
This set down
This: were we led all that way for
Birth or Death? There was a Birth, certainly,
We had evidence and no doubt. I had seen birth and death,
But had thought they were different; this Birth was
Hard and bitter agony for us, like Death, our death.
We returned to our places, these Kingdoms,
But no longer at ease here, in the old dispensation,
With an alien people clutching their gods.
I should be glad of another death.

Conrad Aiken

CHRISTMAS EVE

Between the snowflake and the star
among the falling grains of sand
the interval of near or far
from Avatar to Samarkand

and voices on the midnight blown
and laughter in the sunlight gone
the jewel fallen from a throne
and ashes on a sill at dawn

as of the unseen in the seen
and of the unheard in the heard
the meaning that we almost mean
the truth within the broken word

in these is our epiphany
the pebble on the crucial road
the thorn upon the breaking tree
the back that bends beneath the load

and it is time we turned again
toward the window of the soul
where daybreak brings its sure amen
from the vast vista of the Whole.

Edna St. Vincent Millay

TO JESUS ON HIS BIRTHDAY

For this your mother sweated in the cold,
For this you bled upon the bitter tree:
A yard of tinsel bought and sold;
A paper wreath; a day at home for me.
The merry bells ring out, the people kneel;
Up goes the man of God before the crowd;
With voice of honey and with eyes of steel
He drones your humble gospel to the proud.
Nobody listens. Less than the wind that blows
Are all your words to us you died to save.
O Prince of Peace! O Sharon's dewy Rose!
How mute you lie within your vaulted grave.
    The stone the angel rolled away with tears
    Is back upon your mouth these thousand years.

Archibald MacLeish

Quietness clings to the air.
Quietness gathers the bell
To a great distance.
Listen!
This is the snow.
This is the slow
Chime
The snow
Makes.
It encloses us.
Time in the snow is alone:
Time in the snow is at last,
Is past.

E. E. Cummings

LITTLE TREE

little tree
little silent Christmas tree
you are so little
you are more like a flower

who found you in the green forest
and were you very sorry to come away?
see   i will comfort you
because you smell so sweetly

i will kiss your cool bark
and hug you safe and tight
just as your mother would,
only don't be afraid

look   the spangles
that sleep all the year in a dark box
dreaming of being taken out and allowed to shine,
the balls the chains red and gold the fluffy threads,

put up your little arms
and i'll give them all to you to hold
every finger shall have its ring
and there won't be a single place dark or unhappy

then when you're quite dressed
you'll stand in the window for everyone to see
and how they'll stare!
oh but you'll be very proud

and my little sister and i will take hands
and looking up at our beautiful tree
we'll dance and sing
"Noel Noel"

Mark Van Doren

DIALOGUE IN DECEMBER

In so much dark no light is little.
    But can light be at the end of the year?
Only listen. It will come.
    And put out dying? And put out fear?
Yes, but listen good heart, listen.
    I do, I do—I see, I hear.
That star is enough in this much night.
    It glitters. But a child has cried.
He is the first one in the world.
    Even the old world, that died?
Even the new—he is all the living.
    And all the dead—are they satisfied?

Listen and look—is there any weeping?
    Only for comfort, only for joy.
Only for love. But the child that was crying—
    He is a beautiful, strange boy.
He is little and weak, this lord of the world.
    But oh, too strong, too strong to destroy.

Allen Tate

I I

Ah, Christ, I love you rings to the wild sky
And I must think a little of the past:
When I was ten I told a stinking lie
That got a black boy whipped; but now at last
The going years, caught in an accurate glow,
Reverse like balls englished upon green baize—
Let them return, let the round trumpets blow
The ancient crackle of the Christ's deep gaze.

Deafened and blind, with senses yet unfound,
Am I, untutored to the after-wit
Of knowledge, knowing a nightmare has no sound;
Therefore with idle hands and head I sit
In late December before the fire's daze
Punished by crimes of which I would be quit.

Langston Hughes

CHRISTMAS EVE
Nearing Midnight in New York

The Christmas trees are almost all sold
And the ones that are left go cheap.
The children almost all over town
Have almost gone to sleep.

The skyscraper lights on Christmas Eve
Have almost all gone out.
There's very little traffic,
Almost no one about.

Our town's almost as quiet
As Bethlehem must have been
Before a sudden angel chorus
Sang PEACE ON EARTH!
GOOD WILL TO MEN!

Our old Statue of Liberty
Looks down almost with a smile
As the Island of Manhattan
Awaits the morning of the Child.

Richard Eberhart

SANTA CLAUS IN OAXACA

Nothing seemed so incongruous
In this Christian country of Indians
In bright clothes, Indians part Spanish,
And tourists neither Indian nor Spanish,
In the warm dusk in a place of bells
When the cathedral rips again the harsh sound
Of every quarter hour, and then the full hour,
Next to the Marques del Valle Hotel,
And in the square the noisy band goes off
Like a jubilant series of firecrackers,
The firecrackers shot off by Mexicans young and old,
Where every breath taken is compassionate,

Nothing seemed so incongruous
As to see Santa Claus in the hot lands
In red cotton garments, trimmed in white,
His bearded face impersonal but appealing,
Walk awkwardly through the square of Oaxaca,
Followed by popping strings of boys and girls,
Mothers with babes mangered in red rebozos.
Where are you going, Santa Claus, walking?
Are you going to the ruins of ancient Mitla?
A gentle Zapotec explains the tombs of Mitla.
This Zapotec survives, but gone is the last fierce Aztec.
Are you hastening to see where the future would go?

Phyllis McGinley

THE BALLAD OF BEFANA
An Epiphany Legend

Befana the Housewife, scrubbing her pane,
Saw three old sages ride down the lane,
Saw three gray travelers pass her door—
Gaspar, Balthazar, Melchior.

"Where journey you, sirs?" she asked of them.
 Balthazar answered, "To Bethlehem,

For we have news of a marvelous thing.
 Born in a stable is Christ the King."

"Give Him my welcome!"
 Then Gaspar smiled,
"Come with us, mistress, to greet the Child."

"Oh, happily, happily would I fare,
Were my dusting through and I'd polished the stair."

 Old Melchior leaned on his saddle horn.
"Then send but a gift to the small Newborn."

"Oh, gladly, gladly I'd send Him one,
 Were the hearthstone swept and my weaving done.

"As soon as ever I've baked my bread,
 I'll fetch Him a pillow for His head,
 And a coverlet too," Befana said.

51

"When the rooms are aired and the linen dry,
I'll look at the Babe."
But the Three rode by.

She worked for a day and a night and a day,
Then, gifts in her hands, took up her way.
But she never could find where the Christ Child lay.

And still she wanders at Christmastide,
Houseless, whose house was all her pride,

Whose heart was tardy, whose gifts were late;
Wanders, and knocks at every gate,
Crying, "Good people, the bells begin!
Put off your toiling and let love in."

Robert Penn Warren

THE LITTLE WHITE HOUSE

The sun of July beats down on the little white house.
The pasture is brown-bright as brass, and like brass sings,
But I stand there, the hills shudder blue and
      withdraw into their dazed distance,
Like paranoia. And the child's cry comes from the house.

Tell me, O where, in what state, did I see the little white house
Which I see—and the wax-wing's gold beak slices
      the blue cedar berry,
Which is as blue as distance. The river, far off, shrinks
Among the hot boulders, no glister, looks dead as a discarded
      snake-skin scrubbed off on stone. The house

Swims in the dazzle of no-Time. Like joy, the child's cry—
      yes, listen—comes from the house.

W. H. Auden

CHORUS OF
ANGELS

Unto you a Child,
A Son is given.
Praising, proclaiming
The ingression of Love,
Earth's darkness invents
The blaze of Heaven,
And frigid silence
Meditates a song;
For great joy has filled
The narrow and the sad,
While the emphasis
Of the rough and big,
The abiding crag
And wandering wave,
Is on forgiveness:
Sing Glory to God
And good-will to men,
All, all, all of them.
Run to Bethlehem.

Paul Engle

CHRISTMAS

In that dark season when all green things die
Christ gave his first live human cry,
Winter that kills the leaf and piles the snow
Brought the small Son of life to grow.
Recall, in the freezing touch of time, men told
That God became a living Child and shook with cold.
Now through our cities bells in their rocking motion
Call to this day their bronze devotion.
Now look! The air, as if the great sky fell,
Shakes all around us. Like a bell
Hung out in glittering space, the whole live earth
Swings and rings in the stars to praise one little birth.

Winfield Townley Scott
POEM AT CHRISTMAS

The lilac bushes were small with winter.
Rain-repeated, the abacus of barberries
Ran red, ran red above the smoking snow
And the green chickweed where it winked.
Low to the ground, fog hovered and blew and shifted.
The house we passed was three miles from the last
And, as it turned out, three miles from the next.
A back road between cold-blackened pines
On a cellar of a morning near December's end.
Nobody visible at the house. My question was
Whom were all the Christmas signals for—
The candles in the windows and the doorwreath
Ribboned to render hemlock a gay creation?
At most a stranger or two passed once a day,
Like us, in a moment passing. For us, then?
Yes, if we happened by. But of necessity
First for the mingled joy of decoration
And whoever made it. How else could it be?

May Sarton

NATIVITY
Piero Della Francesca

O cruel cloudless space,
And pale bare ground where the poor infant lies!
Why do we feel restored
As in a sacramental place?
Here Mystery is taking place
And here a vision of such peace is stored
Healing flows from it through our eyes.

Comfort and joy are near,
Not as we know them in the usual ways,
Personal and expected,
But utterly distilled and spare
Like a cool breath upon the air.
Emotion, it would seem, has been rejected
For a clear geometric praise.

Even the angels' stance
Is architectural in form,
And they tell no story.
We see on each grave countenance,
Withheld as in a formal dance,
The awful joy, the serene glory:
It is the inscape keeps us warm.

Poised as a monument,
Thought rests, and in these balanced spaces

Images meditate;
Whatever Piero meant,
The strange impersonal does not relent:
Here is love, naked, lying in great state
On the bare ground, as in all human faces.

Karl Shapiro

CHRISTMAS TREE

Because the tree is joyous and as a child
Lovely in posture, fresh as wind to smell,
Bearing clear needles like a coat of hair,
    And is well-combed and always mild,
      And stands in time so well,
And strong in the forest or beside a tomb
Looks over time and nature everywhere—
Lift it up lightly, bring it in the room.

And for the adoring man, and long ago
The adoring man who was obscure and clean,
Bring in the tree and stand it on the block.
    He felt that he was free to go;
      He stood beneath the green.
Going was freedom, freedom under the tree,
Freedom before the last crow of the cock,
And life exchanged to keep his freedom free.

Summer is sweet because it brings outside
The warmth of houses and the heated air;
We lie on grass as on a delightful rug.
    Christmas brings winter like a bride
      Indoors with white to wear.
The tree looks normal in the house; it grows
Swiftly into the floor; the children hug
The visitor with his dark and pretty clothes.

Silver and gold and mirror-bright and red,
Now hang the egg-shell baubles on the bough

With tinsel hair as shimmering as a dress,
     And one white star upon his head,
          Proud as a Roman now;
And toys, the miniature instruments of pride,
Lay underneath with packages to bless
The material kingdom of the eternal bride.

Between the acquisiton and the prayer
These stand more human for the common days;
The fir, the family, and the pungent wreath
     And one poinsettia like a crimson flare.
          I think the history of praise
Is central in this present-flowering green
That breathes on little children underneath
And keeps them like the infant Nazarene.

John Frederick Nims

CHRISTMAS TREE

This seablue fir that rode the mountain storm
Is swaddled here in splints of tin to die.
Sofas around like toads of velvet swarm
And spidery cabinets glitter with flat eye,
For lacquer in the branches runs like rain
And resin of treasure starts from every vein.

Light is a dancer here and cannot rest.
No tanagers or jays are half so bright
As swarms of fire that deep in fragrance nest
In jungles of the gilt exotic night
Where melons hang like moonstone. White above
Rises that perfect star, the sign of love.

On carpets' fairy turf, in rainbow dark,
Here once the enchanted children laid their heads,
Reached for the floating moon above the park,
And all their hopes were simple blues and reds.
Beneath the electric halo, none could see
Swords in the ankle of the victim tree.

Each named a patron star: Arthur said green
For August in the country; and Betty blue
For swinging and the Florida surf; while Jeanne
Decided gold. One horoscope was true:
The star of Donald low and lava-red—
Impetuous Donald, in Australia dead.

Our lives were bound to sorcery and night.
Zodiacs crumble on the boughs of rust
For every child is gone. Some burned too bright
And now lie broken in the bins of dust;
And some, a fortunate few, adventured far
And found assurance in the perfect star.

William Stafford

DECEMBER TWENTY-FIVE

The date is ashamed. After all these years
to come to this! The bells deny
themselves, in a hurry to have a new trial. Wrong!—
Christmas was one day and not again.
The only thing that lasts is when you die.

Clocks may cross themselves: they are right just once,
no matter how often they assert a return;
and our sky knows this, no matter what bells, what song.
Still, the next thing leads toward the last, wherever
that is, and nothing is right so far, we learn

From the bells. Well, any judgment, if it is right,
honors its day; and sight depends on the eye
to bring truth. So go ahead—ring the bells long
all over the world: maybe they will sound, after all,
this time, in the right part of the sky.

Randall Jarrell

THE AUGSBURG ADORATION

Mozart, Goethe, and the Duke of Wellington
Spent the night at the Drei Mohren; so did we.
Did the Duke of Wellington find by his bed
Two bananas and two sugar-cubes, as we did?
Did the sparrows cheep, cheep, cheep to get the sugar?

And did Mozart sleep, next night, beside the highest
Spire in all the world — unfinished then? Ulm's emblem
Is a sparrow holding in its beak a straw.
You can buy it, in chocolate, at the bakeries.

Did Goethe see, among the cobblestones, the Roman
Manhole-covers marked S P Q R? For the breath
Of those letters, the Senate and the People
Lived for us, indomitable as the sparrows
The bread-eating cats stalked in the ruins of Rome.

Travellers, we come to Rome, Ulm, Augsburg,
To adore something: the child nursing at the stone
Breast beside a stone ox, stone ass, a flesh-and-blood
Sparrow who nests in the manger. The Three Kings
Bring him stones and stones and stones, the sparrow
Brings a straw. The years have worn away the stone,
But the bird cramming food into the beseeching
Mouth in its nest of rubbish, is as perfect
As when the child first said of Mozart, Goethe,
And the Iron Duke: *One of them shall not fall*
On the ground without your Father. They have fallen
And the sparrow has not fallen. The straw-bearing

Sparrow at Ulm, at Augsburg, is indistinguishable
In its perfection from the sparrow who brought straw
To its nest, food to its young, in Rome, in Nazareth —
The green Forum's sparrows are the sparrows of home.

Chad Walsh

God is abroad tonight.
Let all good people stay indoors
While, map in satchel, He explores
    The city of His sight.

Pull down the window shade,
For it is best to picture only
The point of light that hovers lonely
    In alleys that we laid.

He knocks on door to door
But cannot knock at all there are.
The city reaches very far.
    Hold your head firm to the floor.

Sometimes by waiting, win.
Or win at least a night's reprieve.
And with the dawn He'll surely leave.
    But lock the darkness in.

Thomas Merton

CAROL

Flocks feed by darkness with a noise of whispers,
In the dry grass of pastures,
And lull the solemn night with their weak bells.

The little towns upon the rocky hills
Look down as meek as children:
Because they have seen come this holy time.

God's glory, now, is kindled gentler than low candlelight
Under the rafters of a barn:
Eternal Peace is sleeping in the hay,
And Wisdom's born in secret in a straw-roofed stable.

And O! Make holy music in the stars, you happy angels.
You shepherds, gather on the hill.
Look up, you timid flocks, where the three kings
Are coming through the wintry trees;

While we unnumbered children of the wicked centuries
Come after with our penances and prayers,
And lay them down in the sweet-smelling hay
Beside the wise men's golden jars.

Robert Lowell

CHRISTMAS EVE UNDER
HOOKER'S STATUE

Tonight a blackout. Twenty years ago
I hung my stocking on the tree, and hell's
Serpent entwined the apple in the toe
To sting the child with knowledge. Hooker's heels
Kicking at nothing in the shifting snow,
A cannon and a cairn of cannon balls
Rusting before the blackened Statehouse, know
How the long horn of plenty broke like glass
In Hooker's gauntlets. Once I came from Mass;

Now storm-clouds shelter Christmas, once again
Mars meets his fruitless star with open arms,
His heavy saber flashes with the rime,
The war-god's bronzed and empty forehead forms
Anonymous machinery from raw men;
The cannon on the Common cannot stun
The blundering butcher as he rides on Time—
The barrel clinks with holly. I am cold:
I ask for bread, my father gives me mould;

His stocking is full of stones. Santa in red
Is crowned with wizened berries. Man of war,
Where is the summer's garden? In its bed
The ancient speckled serpent will appear,
And black-eyed susan with her frizzled head.
When Chancellorsville mowed down the volunteer,

"All wars are boyish," Herman Melville said;
But we are old, our fields are running wild:
Till Christ again turn wanderer and child.

Raymond Roseliep

KODACHROME:
CHRISTMAS EVE

We hadn't finished riddling
Marianne Moore and just how
mind's an *intractable thing*,
or given our oyster stew

a chance to settle, or climbed
our gift hill, when a neighbor
dropped in 'just for a second'
to capture us in color.

There we still sit: my mother's
bluegown deeper than distance,
my blacksuit somehow darker
by bayberry light and crèche,

query left quiet as birth
or star my brother had cut
to honor a boy's first breath.
No wind has fractured that night

or mind enduring, enthralled.
My mother's lifted finger
poises above the tinseled
ribbon locking as a door.

Gwendolyn Brooks

CHRISTMAS AT CHURCH

The organ thunders, murmurs, is complete,
    Is hallowed, melts in mysteries.
No more the troubles of the day or dusk
When music is a leaning wall of peace.

We abide in beauty. Beneath high-vaulted glory
The Christmas message is a Medicine.
A healing lotion for offended eyes.
An ointment for the ache that freezes in.

This is our refuge and our Strengthener,
To gird us, spur us back into the flame
And steam. Our forces, faith and confidence.
Our guide, the superstructure of a Name.

Edwin Honig

KING OF DEATH

I

December winds knock down a shutter. Bronze
evening roughens, rusting toward the town.
Sprung in darkness, he comes alive to search
the lowdown neighborhood for witnesses.

Stretched bare, the ransacked town turns in at nine.
Fire bells halloo him past
the empty depots — feints, beckonings
toward surrender, almost try his mind.

He sees a misty soldier on the way,
warring with rocks on window-glass,
fall and crash, the swelling sirens
pouring by him featureless.

Run swift, run slow, in shadow safeties click
on dumb revolvers; his long stretch narrows
down to stand their muzzles' hollowness
before they bellow darkness out.

The papers later said no witnesses
appeared, though faces peered all night
behind the blinds, shifting from TV sets
to nonstop hysterical patrol cars.

II

After all, he had, and possibly,
when every gobbet's gathered up,
will still appear to have (maimed
man's king of death and poverty)
    extraordinary life.
    Death is what can die,
    in every man, at last.

Awakenings are naked, tremorous,
a waiting to be taken, murderer
or bride, to heart; pursuer sought,
mistaken, shadowing himself;
    feared, a fury silenced,
    darting to sacrifice;
    forsaken, a presence past.

III

Toward cockcrow, when the inexhaustible poor
lay down and slept, some paid eyewitnesses,
just for the record, detailed an expiration.

They said the howling ceased, a calm descended.
A groggy soldier rose and walked off stiffly
in a borrowed coat. The hill began to shapen

Where the stripped and cornered victim crept,
just as, from his riddled sides, a glory woke
and blazed. It shook, amazing and amazed —

as if enraged, as if it would not die.

Howard Nemerov

SANTA CLAUS

Somewhere on his travels the strange Child
Picked up with this overstuffed confidence man,
Affection's inverted thief, who climbs at night
Down chimneys, into dreams, with this world's
    goods.
Bringing all the benevolence of money,
He teaches the innocent to want, thus keeps
Our fat world rolling. His prescribed costume,
White flannel beard, red belly of cotton waste,
Conceals the thinness of essential hunger,
An appetite that feeds on satisfaction;
Or, pregnant with possessions, he brings forth
Vanity and the void. His name itself
Is corrupted, and even Saint Nicholas, in his turn,
Gives off a faint and reminiscent stench,
The merest soupçon, of brimstone and the pit.

Now, at the season when the Child is born
To suffer for the world, suffer the world,
His bloated Other, jovial satellite
And sycophant, makes his appearance also
In a glitter of goodies, in a rock candy glare.
Played at the better stores by bums, for money,
This annual savior of the economy
Speaks in the parables of the dollar sign:
Suffer the little children to come to Him.

At Easter, he's anonymous again,
Just one of the crowd lunching on Calvary.

74

Richard Wilbur

A CHRISTMAS HYMN

A stable-lamp is lighted
Whose glow shall wake the sky;
The stars shall bend their voices,
And every stone shall cry.
And every stone shall cry,
And straw like gold shall shine;
A barn shall harbor heaven,
A stall become a shrine.

This child through David's city
Shall ride in triumph by;
The palm shall strew its branches,
And every stone shall cry.
And every stone shall cry,
Though heavy, dull, and dumb,
And lie within the roadway
To pave his kingdom come.

Yet he shall be forsaken,
And yielded up to die;
The sky shall groan and darken,
And every stone shall cry.
And every stone shall cry
For stony hearts of men:
God's blood upon the spearhead,
God's love refused again.

But now, as at the ending,
The low is lifted high;
The stars shall bend their voices,
And every stone shall cry.
And every stone shall cry
In praises of the child
By whose descent among us
The worlds are reconciled.

Howard Moss

AT THE FIRE FOUNTAIN
Christmas, Radio City

The season's casualty of squandered green,
The totem of the wood, symbolic pine,
Is cut and raised to be brought down again.
The twisted wreath that emulates a crown
Of thorns hangs up its Christ, the blood-red berry;
What blood once ran true scarlet in the vein
Runs now to crooked waste: the inventory

Gathered in a thousand squares of light,
Where all the sudden wealth we get and give
(As if the season were a safety vault)
Is but the gold exchange of how we live.
The same cold knuckles grate the shuttered door,
The same sad visionaries still endure
Poverty, the occupation of the poor.

Here, the fountain's question marks of haze
No longer glaze the marble. Winter's spare,
Bone monuments of stone and glass appraise
Themselves across the plaza, the evening air
Holds up the starlight in that silent, queer
Moment of perfection when each thing assays
Its selfhood only, and perception stays.

Diagonal Prometheus, gilded, bare,
Strains his hard gold body and gold hair
To flight that trembles in an abstract fire;
A pine is centered in a tent of wire

Above his head, and as the tongue-tied hour
Breaks upon the bells, the season's martyr
Merges with the vision of the fire-bringer

To burn two parables to one: The rack
Whose nails of fire pierced the hanging Jesus
Blazes as that stone where chained Prometheus
Suffered the vital eagle coming back.
The portents of this night ascend to mourn
Our deaths in theirs; on two crossed sticks, on stone,
By thorn or beak, in anguish, Gods are born.

James Dickey

So much of life is spent driving,
So much in small towns
In the dusk, where one stops,
Puts a dime in a parking meter,
And saunters, invisible, among
These particular strangers.
There are some times when this is

At Christmas, in a town in south Alabama,

And, hanging over the streets
On wires, are green bunting, many old
Decorations, some plastic new ones as well,
Brittle, well-meaning, and wrong.
The sun at the end of the main street
Is dull red, and puts a bright red
On all the faces seen once.

One wishes to stroll all the way

Into the sun, but the town will not last,
Though down by the railroad station
The gaiety does not diminish.
You are in one of the Christmas towns
With the store-haunting clean country children,
Enchanted by the colors that come out
Of town-hall attics and fire departments and soar

Over their heads once a year:

79

Strangers may also know them, who spend,
For space and time to be here —
To walk under flowering rags,
A warm winter sun in their eyes —
Only ten silver cents in a lifetime.
This buys a lot on this day:
Warmth for both hands outside

The pockets, a forehead crimson

With the first dark, a silence in oneself
Amongst the countrified noise,
A feeling of having bathed in secret
Inside one's clothes: an hour
To be unnoticed and ghostlike,
Clear-eyed, damp-haired and smiling
And awestruck by the legends of the race.

Vassar Miller

Sleep, my beloved, under the hay,
Under the straw, under the snow,
Under the wings of the dark and the day,
Of the meadowlark and the crow.

Sleep, my beloved, under the straw,
Under the snow, under the hay,
Under the long arms of grace and of law,
With a lullaby and a ballet.

Sleep, my beloved, under the snow,
Under the hay, under the straw,
Under the sky and earth below,
The same light that the shepherds saw.

Philip Booth

UNCLE CHRISTMAS

Christmas is like a dentist coming for breakfast,
arriving (before the family has brushed) with presents
wrapped by professionals, riddled with family jokes.

The children, who pray release from daily check-ups,
have loved him for lollypop weeks. Braced by tinsel,
they empty their socks to hang for this fat uncle:

he promises pearls, if his nieces, toward this one day,
will grace their meals and promise to fight decay.
You'd think it was his birthday, the way we light

old candles, and set up ritual equipment all night.
Even before the streetlights dim, we wake to welcome
his coming: this gifted doctor descended into The Home

(a human bazaar more bizarre than Persians or Turks).
But this is one day when Dentistry actually works:
we breakfast on prophylaxis, lifted, together,

above the bad breath which corrupts our most loving acts.
The children love him. Only we parents (for Christ's sake)
fear the price of this day he extracts.

Donald Hall

CHRISTMAS EVE
IN WHITNEYVILLE
To my father

December, and the closing of the year;
The momentary carolers complete
Their Christmas Eves, and quickly disappear
Into their houses on each lighted street.

Each car is put away in each garage;
Each husband home from work, to celebrate,
Has closed his house around him like a cage,
And wedged the tree until the tree stood straight.

Tonight you lie in Whitneyville again,
Near where you lived, and near the woods or farms
Which Eli Whitney settled with the men
Who worked at mass-producing firearms.

The main-street, which was nothing after all
Except a school, a stable, and two stores,
Was improvised and individual,
Picking its way alone, until the wars.

Now Whitneyville is like the other places,
Ranch-houses stretching flat beyond the square,
Same stores and movie, same composite faces
Speaking the language of the public air.

Old buildings loiter by this cemetery.
When you were twelve, they dressed you up in black

83

With five companions from the class, to carry
The body of a friend. Now you are back,

Beside him, but a man of fifty-two.
Talk to the boy. Tell him about the years
When Whitneyville quadrupled, and how you
And all his friends went on to make careers,

Had cars as long as hayricks, boarded planes,
For Rome and Paris where the pace was slow,
And took the time to think how yearly gains,
Profit and volume made the business grow.

"The things you had to miss," you said last week,
"Or thought you had to, take your breath away."
You propped yourself on pillows, where your cheek
Was hollow, stubbled lightly with new gray.

This love is jail; another sets us free.
Tonight the houses and their noise distort
The thin rewards of solidarity.
The houses lean together for support.

The noises fail. Now lights go on upstairs.
The men and women are undressing now
To go to sleep. They put their clothes on chairs
To take them up again. I think of how,

Across America, when midnight comes,
They lie together and are quieted,
To sleep as children sleep, who suck their thumbs,
Cramped in the narrow rumple of each bed.

They will not have unpleasant thoughts tonight.
They make their houses jails, and they will take
No risk of freedom for the appetite,
Or knowledge of it, when they are awake.

The lights go out and it is Christmas Day.
The stones are white, the grass is black and deep;
I will go back and leave you here to stay,
While the dark houses harden into sleep.

Daniel Hughes

A LIST OF SOME NAMES AND PLACES OF ABODE OF THOSE IN WHOSE MIND THE LIGHT OF GOD HAS ARISEN OR IS GRACIOUSLY ARISING

In New Hampshire: a woman who has not travelled widely,
Who guides the very young, who bears the calumnious stir
Of a different way of life, whose mind shreds superstition,
Who waits with patience for the Giant Forms: Teresa.

In Rhode Island: a man who for twenty years had pondered
The right rebellion, who attacks now that his sword is honed,
The purifications ready, the armies advancing,
Who will walk among the slain with sorrow and dismay: Dave.

In New York: a beauty, contained in her goings, from mirrors
In a quick retreat withdrawing, tender of the glass,
Who dances out her love in exotic gardens, the wells
Where God's best idea lances her fragrant spring: Karen.

In California: a man who drains all books for their spoil,
To mean more, to mean more, like the holy babbling of the bush,
No covenant withdrawn, no image past redemption —
To mean, that the human burn to his most lucid Verb: Lou.

In Michigan: a wife, wholly met and vulnerable,
Who sketches her nakedness before her mirror's silence,

That her body's puzzle become her generous choice, bringing,
Say, cheese and wine to her laboring spouse: Mary.

In Siena, an old man. I look upon these envelopes
For his small, blue hand. I see the shining fields
Where he drinks from ancient glass the finest Tuscan water.
I see him travel beneath the singing towers of the Lord: Léllo.

Sing Praises!

Bruce Cutler

DECEMBER TWENTY-FIFTH
ON THE RIO GRANDE

It is what rises, draws together, grows
around an appetite of dust, breaks out
along the pewter facings of the air

what falls through roaring atmospheres of light

what greens mesquite, humps the bunch grass

what drags itself across the face of flint
and sinks in mountain seams of sulphur

what drives itself through iron, through gold, and down
to tilting marble beds above the dikes
of final lava. and then returns,
takes back each crystal filament, sweats along
the hard saguaro root, wakens the grub,
drums the sleeping prairie dog to deeper dark,

bending, bending, until it springs again
through sand, consuming air, gnawing the light

and it is one, one water, one river
flowing out of the jagged banks of birth
flowing under the arches of our years

as it rises, draws together, grows
around an appetite of dust ...

George Starbuck

DECEMBER POEM FOR JUNE

At the least scrape laid open (and shouldn't they be ashamed?)
to the ripe chalk of their hearts (but they are all heart) four angels
puff at their golden trumpets, promise-crammed
like cornucopias of cotton candy.

Behind them, and of the selfsame gilded stuff
as the Statehouse, shepherds, kings, and some hard-shell sheep
sully, so poets say (and they ought to know) the steep
Common the shovels have sliced for us like divinity fudge,

where a friend of a friend of mine once (I was that close to it) ran
hobbling the blackest lamb in his woolly arms, and ran
until a patrolman nailed him and sent him up-
and-over to Joy Street Station to simmer down.

But they are good plaster creatures. They only
dream (as we all of us dream) a miraculous day
of Spirits spiriting wiseman and shepherd away,
bringing for every plaster angel his plastered Angel.

Lewis Turco

THE GLASS NEST

The angel hair of winter — come down to
Spring from the Feast of the Nativity —
lies among crocus under the lilac:
a moss of spun glass among spears of green
and cream. Pendulous upon a limb, seed
and suet dangle in the wind straining
through the straining bush: a roof of birds.
Nuthatch and black-capped chickadee, grackle
and cowbird — white with grey, black upon brown —
move among the branches and the sunlight
(like a bright ladder for wings) which coaxes
life out of the bark in furious buds.

The snow has melted, all but the false snow,
filaments spun from silica, mica
ice made for a metal tree topped by a
star of tinsel whose light was wired to our
wall. Carpets and curtains between us and
the wind, winter's emblem glistened above
gifts no Magi could have dreamt in their sands
or tamarinds: glistened for a space.
                                        Now
the birds come tearing the angel hair, their
eyes bright with birth. Our useless artifice
shall make a glass nest in a real tree. Its
dangle will be rare among sunlight and
showers, leaves, limbs, explosions of true wings.